Signs and Symbols

Clive Pace and Jean Birch

Published by Collins Educational
London and Glasgow
First Impression 1990

Series Editor Pat Green

Typeset in Great Britain by Kalligraphics Ltd., Horley, Surrey
Printed and bound in Great Britain

Acknowledgements
Frances Pace: page 5 (top and bottom left), page 6 (bottom), page 6 (all),
page 16 (all), page 21 (top), page 22 (top left and centre right)
Clive Pace: page 5 (top centre, top right, centre right, bottom right),
page 6 (top and right), page 7 (all), page 8 (all), page 9 (all), page 12
(all), page 13, page 14, page 15 (top), page 17 (all), page 18 (bottom),
page 19 (bottom), page 20 (right), page 21 (bottom), page 22 (bottom),
page 23 (left)
Jean Birch: page 10, page 11 (all), page 15 (bottom), page 18 (top), page 19
(top), page 20 (left), page 22 (top right), page 23 (top and bottom right)

Contents

Introduction

If you look you will see signs and symbols all around you. Signs tell us where to go, what to do and what not to do. They tell us the names of places, of streets and of shops. Sometimes they warn us of dangers.

This book tells you about different signs and symbols which you can see every day.

Signs without words

These signs have no words.
The pictures show what they mean.

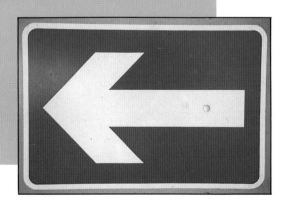

Signs with words

Some signs use words.

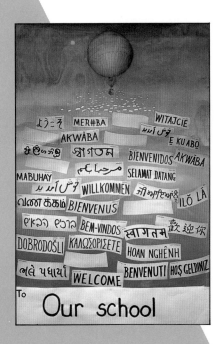

Some people don't use English as their main language so some signs are in two languages.

Road Signs

Road signs are different shapes and sizes.
They **give** information **to** drivers.

Signs shaped like
triangles give warnings.
Signs shaped like circles
tell drivers what to do.

Signs that give directions

Some signs show us the way to other towns.

Some signs show us the way to places in our own town.

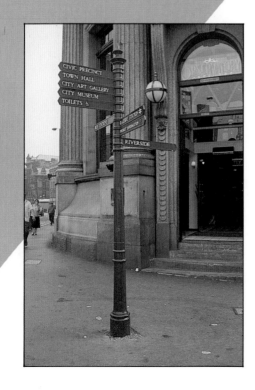

11

Street signs

Every street has its own name.
Street signs tell you where you are.

In some towns there is a number on the sign. This shows the district. It also appears as part of the postcode.

Information signs

This sign shows where
visitors to a town can
get *information*.

Maps like this tell them where there are interesting places. This sign gives information about a park.

Warning signs

Warning

Do not trespass
on the Railway
Penalty £200

Some signs tell us not to
do things.
They warn us to be
careful.

DANGER OF DEATH
KEEP OFF

NO SMOKING
IN THESE SEATS

These signs warn
burglars to keep away.

Public House Signs

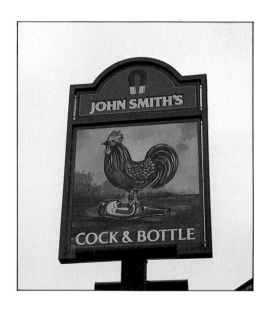

Pubs often have very interesting signs.

The signs which hang outside them usually have pictures that go with the names.

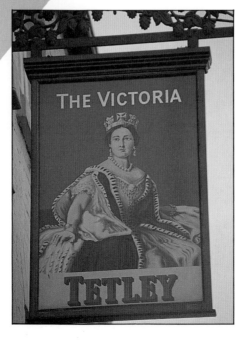

Ciphers, symbols and coats of arms

The initials on this post box are called the cipher of Queen Victoria.
This crown is the symbol of the Royal Mail.

These coats of arms are also symbols which we use from the past.

Car signs and shop signs

Cars have to have
number plates.
They are white at the
front of the car and
yellow at the back.
The car makers put their
own special signs on
their cars.

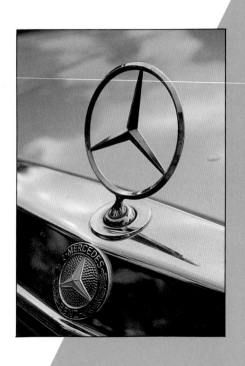

Sometimes shops use interesting signs to show what they sell.

Glossary

Cipher   Initials

Coat of arms   A family sign which people used
                  to decorate their shields.

District   An area of a town.

Information   Facts we need to know.

Postcode   The letters and numbers which
                  are the last line of an address.
                  The postcode helps the Post
                  Office deliver the letters.

Symbol   A special sign which stands for
                  something.

Index